ZENKI
WAY

the ZENKi WAY

A Guide to Designing & Enjoying Your Own Creative Softies

Trixi Symonds

SCHIFFER PUBLISHING

4880 Lower Valley Road • Atglen, PA 19310

Published by Schiffer Publishing, Ltd.
4880 Lower Valley Road
Atglen, PA 19310
Phone: (610) 593-1777; Fax: (610) 593-2002
E-mail: Info@schifferbooks.com
Web: www.schifferbooks.com

For our complete selection of fine books on this and related
subjects, please visit our website at www.schifferbooks.com.
You may also write for a free catalog.

Schiffer Publishing's titles are available at special discounts for
bulk purchases for sales promotions or premiums. Special
editions, including personalized covers, corporate imprints,
and excerpts, can be created in large quantities for special
needs. For more information, contact the publisher.

We are always looking for people to write books on new and
related subjects. If you have an idea for a book, please contact
us at proposals@schifferbooks.com.

ZENKIS ARE NOT
JUST SOFT ON THE
OUTSIDE, THEY'RE SOFT ON
THE INSIDE TOO. THEY ARE
SWEET SOFT-HEARTED
FAITHFUL FRIENDS WHO'LL
ALWAYS STAND BY YOU.

CONTENTS

INTRODUCING ZENKIS AND THE ZENKI WAY

For many years now, my life has been driven by a desire to teach people around the world to sew. In the last few years in particular, this activity has become almost all-encompassing. Especially since I founded Sew a Softie in 2016.

The success of Sew a Softie's global events has inspired me to make my own approach to designing softies accessible to everyone and anyone who wants to sew with groups or kids. I call this approach the zenki way, and I call the softies zenkis.

So, what is a zenki? And what is the zenki way of sewing softies?

I think this whole book is the best answer to these questions. Still, I would like to say a few short words about how the zenkis came about and why I think they're so special.

Perhaps you'll be disappointed when I confess that zenkis and the zenki way have absolutely nothing to do with Zen. My first zenki was originally called Zenkidu, a name suggested by an old Babylonian epic, of all things. The hero of that epic has a friend and faithful companion called Enkidu. I really liked that name and called my first zenki-style softie Zenkidu, which was soon shortened to Zenki.

Now, Zenki was not just an ordinary softie. Zenki was the simplest softie in the world. Probably in the entire universe. At least, that's what I saw every time I looked at him.

Pretty soon I was busy making new zenki-style softies. They required just two pieces of felt, a simple running stitch, and . . . well, nothing much else. I found myself taking part in a kind of softie evolution and watching how new varieties of zenkis evolved. Zenki was no longer just the personal name of a single lovable softie. It had become the name for *a whole new kind of softie.*

So, this book is about zenkis and the zenki way of making a softie. It's about how to make the simplest softies in the world. And it's about how to think in the zenki way. I hope that when you've made the zenkis in this book, you too will feel inspired to go off and design your very own zenkis.

If sewing softies with kids or groups strikes you as an impossible dream, then my zenkis are here to show you that sewing a softie can be simplicity itself. Or if you think that sewing softies with kids is just too difficult to try, then zenkis are here to show you a new way to go about making a softie.

All we have to do is listen to them.

ABOUT TOOLS AND MATERIALS

One rule I always find myself saying is, check that your tools and materials do the job well. Choose whatever you want, then test them out. If you do this, you can't go wrong.

Felt

All the zenkis in this book are made with felt. It's soft, it's easy to sew, it comes in amazing colors, and it doesn't fray. There are acrylics, wool blends, pure wools, and even bamboo felts. The main thing is to check that the felt you choose is easy to sew. Some felts are stiff, which makes pushing a needle through a bit difficult, especially for young sewers.

Needles

Any needle that works is a good needle. People often believe that large blunt needles are best for kids. I'd disagree. If you can't sew with it, neither can a child. Small hands are well suited to ordinary sewing needles, and I think that they need them in order to have an easy, enjoyable sewing experience.

There are more needles out there than stars in the night. I like to use small chenille needles, sizes 18 through 24. The smaller chenille, which is the 24, has a smaller eye. It's great for ordinary sewing thread. If you're sewing with a thicker thread, like embroidery floss, then you'll need to use one of the larger chenille needles, say a size 18 or 20, which have larger eyes.

Thread

All the zenkis in this book are made with ordinary sewing thread. With my students, I like to double the thread and knot the ends so it doesn't slip off their needle. Watch out for cheap threads. They're often poor in quality and break easily, usually right in the middle of sewing. I use Aurifil thread. It's highquality and a pleasure to sew with. Also, I like the people at Aurifil. They've supported Sew a Softie for years by donating wonderful boxes of threads to Sew a Softie participants.

Pins

You'll need pins to hold two layers of felt together so they don't move while you're sewing. And if you think that pins are just pins, think again. Clover is a Japanese company that makes beautiful, high-quality pins that slip in and out of felt effortlessly.

If you don't want to use pins with your kids, you can try using sewing clips. These are plastic clips with no sharp pointy bits and can be purchased at sewing-supply stores. Clover sells these as "wonder clips."

Stuffing

Zenkis are softies and will need something soft inside them.

Anything soft will do. Mostly I use polyester fiberfill, but it doesn't make a huge difference what stuffing you use. What does make a difference is *how* you stuff your softie. When stuffing, make sure you pull off smallish tufts of stuffing rather than grabbing it in big wads. If the tufts are too large, the softie will feel and look lumpy.

Oh, and I should warn you: kids go crazy with stuffing. They delight in stuffing that softie and often believe that the more stuffing they can push in, the better their softie will be. In my workshops, I am not infrequently called to perform emergency surgery on some poor softie who is exploding under the pressure of his or her own insides.

Weighting Material

Sometimes I use a weighting material to give a zenki weight to sit or stand by itself.

I like to use rice grains, but any dry, granular material such as lentils, dried peas, or sand will do the job. Some people prefer to use plastic pellets in order to avoid the possibility of attracting critters like weevils.

Scissors

It's good to have a pair of fabric scissors that cut well. This goes for scissors that young kids use too. Kiddy scissors are not suited to cutting felt. Fiskars and Kai are two companies that make good-quality small-sized fabric scissors suitable for kids to hold and use.

You should also know that if you use your fabric scissors to cut paper, they will become blunt and cease to cut fabric cleanly.

Last, it can be fun to have a pair of pinking shears. These are scissors that make a zigzag cut, which is a simple way to suggest all sorts of things, like a toothy mouth. I bought a pair of Clover scissors that cut with a beautiful scalloped edge last time I was in New York. They were something I couldn't buy in Australia. That was twenty-five years ago now, and those scissors still cut like new. Just goes to show: a good pair of scissors can be a pleasure for life, or at least for quite a few decades.

Glue

Not all glues are created equal. The surface of felt is made up of tiny hairs, and many glues have difficulty binding to it. The only way to know if a glue binds well to felt is by trial and error. I use a Bostik glue stick, but it's not available in all countries. Thick, tacky glues can work well on felt, but PVA glues tend to be runny and dry very slowly, which can be a nightmare when making projects with kids.

If you're having trouble finding a suitable glue, you can opt for a low-temperature glue gun. A glue gun can apply glue in small, precise blobs, and they dry quickly. Just be aware that the nozzle gets hot. It will burn skin that touches it, so young children should not use this tool unsupervised.

And remember, glue is really just a convenient shortcut. If you're having a hard time finding a working glue, you can always opt to sew the feature on instead.

Marking Tools

This name covers all sorts of pens and pencils that can draw a line on felt.

I use a soft 2B or 3B pencil to mark light-colored felt. Press lightly because lead pencil doesn't always rub off so easily. And if you try to scrub a mark off, you'll damage the surface of your felt.

My all-time favorite marker is a white wax pencil. It's a lifesaver when you need to draw on dark felts, and it rubs off easily and well.

Hole Punch

A hole punch can be really useful for punching out circles of felt.

I use a replaceable hollow punch, which consists of a metal tube with a range of sharpened circular endpieces that you can screw on and off in different sizes. To punch out a circle, I simply place it on the felt and bang it with a hammer. I often use it to make eyes.

TRANSFERRING TEMPLATES

The simplest way to transfer a template onto felt is to cut out the template from paper and trace around it onto your felt. Alternatively, you can use the freezer-paper method. Copy your template onto the paper side of the freezer paper. Place the freezer paper with its shiny side facedown on your felt. Iron the freezer paper onto the felt with a warm iron, which will cause it to stick to the felt. Last, cut around the template and peel the freezerpaper off the felt. That's all there is to it.

ABOUT STITCHES

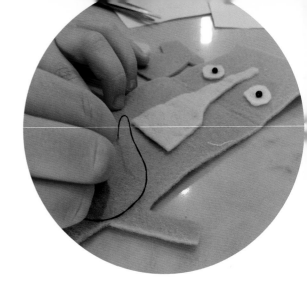

Go to Sew a Softie on YouTube to see my video tutorial for each of these stitches!

Running Stitch

Everyone has seen a running stitch. It looks just like a line of dashes. It's one of my favorite stitches and is really simple to learn. To sew a running stitch, you push your needle up through the fabric from underneath, then push the tip of the needle back through to the underneath side, then push the tip back up again to the top side of the fabric and pull the thread right through. Keep repeating this. When you get used to this stitch, you can start making a few dips in and out before you pull the needle and thread right through on the top side of the fabric.

Cross Stitch

A cross stitch is simply an X shape made from two single stitches. It works well for all sorts of things. I sometimes use it as a belly button. To make a cross stitch, push your needle up through from underneath the fabric and then push the needle and thread back through to the underneath side, making a single stitch on top of the fabric. Repeat this to make a second stich that crosses over the first stitch in an X shape on the top side of the fabric.

French Knot

A French knot is just what it says it is. It's a stitch that makes a little knot. It's pretty easy to do, and once you get the hang of it, you'll love it. To make a French knot, push your needle up through the fabric from underneath, wind your thread around the shaft of your needle, then push your needle back through the fabric to the underneath side. The thread you wound around the shaft of the needle will be left on the top side of the fabric as a knot. I often use a French knot to sew on an eye circle, with the French knot serving as its pupil.

Sewing On a Button

There are an awful lot of buttons around, and they're all different. There's no way I can tell you how to sew on every kind of button. But to sew on an ordinary button with two holes—and four holes will be much the same—is pretty easy.

To sew on a button with two holes, push your needle up through the fabric from underneath the button, passing the needle and thread through one of its holes. Then push the needle back down through the other hole from the top side of the fabric to the underneath side. Repeat this a few times, then make a knot in the thread on the underneath side of the fabric.

RUNNING A ZENKI WORKSHOP

Sewing workshops can be hectic, but it's the nicest kind of hectic.

You may have to become adept at helping students who have sewn their project onto their clothes or completed their softie and forgotten the stuffing. But you'll also be surprised at how well even young children behave when they really want to sew. They know that they are being trusted with items, like needles, usually reserved for adults. And they respond by showing just how sensible and responsible they can be. In all my years of running workshops, they've never disappointed me.

A Matter of Numbers

I'm often asked, How many kids should there be in a workshop? I like to have twenty as a maximum when my daughter, Yiscah, can assist me with students. But if you haven't run a sewing workshop before, I'd set the upper limit at around ten to fifteen. You'll probably be run off your feet, but you should manage. Having said that, smaller groups are the ideal way to begin. If you can, start with five to eight kids. That should allow you time to get to know each student and be able to deal with their needs.

Preparing Yourself

If you're running a workshop, it's a good idea for you, and any assistants, to make the project beforehand. This is by far the best way to understand what a project involves and to get a sense of any difficulties your students might have.

And don't just assume that your tools and supplies will do the job. Check that the thread goes through the eye of the needle you've chosen. Check that scissors cut cleanly and that the glue binds to your fabric.

Problems with tools and supplies make sewing a struggle, especially for kids.

Running the Workshop

I can't tell you how to run a workshop. Not really. Everyone will do it differently. It's a very personal thing. But I can tell you what I like to do in my workshops.

For me, a workshop is always a balancing act between giving guidance and nurturing creativity.

I like to give students maximum freedom to make creative decisions, but enough guidance to make sure they complete their projects all by themselves. In my zenki workshops this is easy to achieve, since zenkis are designed with this in mind.

I also like to get kids working on their project as soon as they arrive. Hanging around isn't the

most interesting start to a workshop, and having kids "on their way" gives me more space to focus on incoming students as they arrive.

I like to be organized. The tables have almost everything the students need to make their zenki, and each table has an example of the zenki that we're making for students to reference.

If you walked in the door, you'd see that in front of each chair is felt for a zenki, with a sewing line drawn on it. As students arrive, they choose the color they like, sit down, and start with designing their zenki's face.

The table will also have bits of colored felt they can cut to make into facial features. In addition, I always have some precut felt shapes. These are great for kids who want to cut out something like a circle that they find difficult to do well. Precut shapes and odd-shaped scraps can also help kids imagine new ways to make their zenki's facial features, not that their imaginations usually need much help.

Their zenki-to-be also has a needle pinned securely into the felt, so that when the time comes to thread their needle it's right there in front of them.

When everyone has arrived, I get the students who have begun making their zenkis' faces to stop work. I explain what we'll be doing and any safety rules. If they haven't sewn before, I will show them how to thread a needle. Then how to do a running stitch, tie a knot, and end their line of sewing.

When students are young, don't expect them to remember what you've said. You'll probably have to remind them how to do these things several times during the workshop. A constant but gentle repetition and encouragement usually does the trick.

Sometimes I place step-by-step instructions on the tables. I find that they can be a useful guide for older students.

When everyone's started sewing, I go around to each student individually to check how they're doing and help them work through any problems.

Also, I always have a handy supply of already-threaded needles for students who might need them. Young students love the challenge of threading needles, but it can be frustrating. I don't want them to feel that they have to get their needles threaded by an adult, but I also don't want threading a needle to become a chore that eclipses the enjoyment and fun of sewing zenkis.

Glue is on the tables unless I'm using a low-temperature glue gun. Then I'll set up a gluing station with an adult assistant or myself to do the gluing. Those low-temperature glue guns have burning-hot nozzles and should not be used by kids without close supervision.

I don't usually put stuffing on their tables. Stuffing is bulky and takes up space. Here, too, I'll set up a stuffing station where students can go to stuff their zenkis. I find it's good to get them off their seats and moving around, and it keeps the workshop buzzing and lively.

Students who finish early can take from the leftover felt and design their own projects. Kids love playing with scraps. They might design pockets to put their zenkis in, accessories, or friends, all sorts of things. Their natural creativity never ceases to impress me. I wish I could bottle it and sip a little every now and then.

TRIXI'S 7 GOLDEN RULES OF SEWING

Unfortunately, this very brief picture of how I run my workshops omits many details. Truth is, there are just too many things that you do to put down in writing.

There are a few stray things, however, that I do want to mention. I call them my 7 Golden Rules of Sewing. I wrote them for parents and teachers seeking a handful of helpful hints on how to sew with groups of young children. You can think of them as a kind of sewing chicken soup: I think they'll help, but even if they don't, they won't hurt.

All Stitches Are Good Stitches

I don't get kids to undo big or messy stitches. I'm happy for them to just get the hang of sewing in a stress-free, supportive atmosphere. I might show them how to get smaller, neater stitches. I might explain that we need small stitches so that stuffing doesn't fall out, but mostly I just let them stitch away. With practice, their stitches do become more controlled and do get smaller and neater.

Let the Kids Make the Decisions

If kids ask my advice on a design matter, I try to encourage them to work out what they think looks good. I want them to think about options and decide what they like. Often children have the idea that an adult can make a better choice. When they begin to trust themselves, they begin to realize that when it comes to sewing, their choices are the ones that matter, not someone else's.

Copying Is Good

When the kids aren't sure how they want to design or go forward with their project, I tell them to look at what other kids in the group are doing to get ideas. It's great for them to look at other people's work for inspiration and to realize that there's nothing wrong with getting ideas from others. Sewing is creative, not competitive.

This Isn't a Race

I always tell the kids that it doesn't matter if they sew slowly or quickly; everyone will finish by the end of the workshop. I want them to enjoy sewing, not to think that finishing first is something they should be striving for.

Every Softie Needs a Baby

I learned this important rule early on. We were sewing koala softies. I shrunk down the template so that early finishers could sew a baby koala

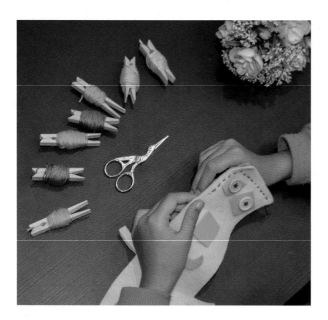

in the time they had left. Well, no one wanted to leave that workshop without a baby koala. There was some frantic sewing going on in the last minutes of that workshop, in order to make sure that their baby koala was finished, with all its decorative touches, before they went home.

Less May Be Good but More Is Much Better

Young children don't like holding back. Try to respect their belief that "more is better." Having said that, I have to admit that there have been times that I have put limits on the sheer number of bows, rhinestones, and so on that some students have wanted to use, in order to still have enough for everyone else in the workshop.

Chocolate Crackles Are a Great Way to End a Workshop

Chocolate crackles are one of those uniquely Australian foods that were a staple at any self-respecting party when I was growing up. I always make a batch for students as an end to my workshops. Everyone knew that those chocolate crackles were coming. Since chocolate crackles are uniquely Australian, this last rule is really: make sure that sewing is something your kids see as fun and exciting.

Trixi's Chocolate Crackle Recipe

Traditional recipes for chocolate crackles have a range of ingredients I don't actually use. My recipe requires only chocolate (very important) and Rice Krispies, which we call Rice Bubbles over here in Australia. I think it's a quicker, easier recipe to make, and according to my students, it's a yummier chocolate crackle to eat.

I prefer to use dark chocolate, but milk chocolate works too. If you're making these with your kids, the fun part, other than licking out the bowl, is decorating them with sprinkles, which we Aussies call hundreds and thousands . . . if you happen to spill them, you'll understand why. Last, I always put my chocolate crackles in the freezer to set. It gives them that extra-special crackle crunch. Okay, here's how you make my chocolate crackles:

Ingredients

- 100g dark chocolate

- 3 cups crisp rice cereal (such as Rice Krispies or Rice Bubbles)

- Sprinkles

1. Melt chocolate.

2. Stir melted chocolate and Rice Krispies together with a wooden spoon until well combined.

3. Spoon mixture into cupcake liners.

4. Decorate with sprinkles.

5. Put in freezer to set.

YOUR BASIC KIT

This is the minimum that you'll need for every project in this book. The felt and any additional supplies you might want to use are listed before each project as additions to your basic kit.

- Needle
- Thread
- Pins or sewing clips
- Stuffing
- Scissors
- Glue
- Marking tool

ZENKi BEGiNNiNGS

You should know that your zenkis can become a little grumpy if you forget to give them a name. Zenkis are very big on names.

SQUARE ZENKI

What You Need in Addition to Your Basic Kit

- Two different-colored 9″ × 9″ squares of felt
- Felt for facial features

Square Zenki was there at the very beginning. Before any other zenkis existed. He was the first. The original zenki. He's very proud of this fact. This is how he came about. A few years ago, I was asked to give a sewing workshop for parents and children at the Australian Museum. The workshop was themed to fit with their Aztec exhibition. I gave them a few designs to choose from. Square Zenki was one of them. The museum chose to go with another project, but Square Zenki had caught my attention. I sensed something unusual in him. He was really simple and yet bursting with creative potential. He's never let me down. He has remained simple but always surprising. Perhaps he still has a bit of Aztec in him.

1. Draw a 5″ square in the center of one of the 9″ × 9″ felt squares. This will be your sewing line.

2. Cut out facial features from felt. Position and glue into place.

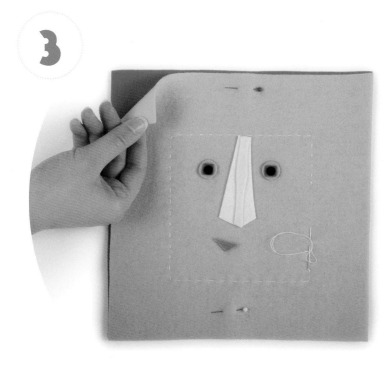

3. Pin the two squares of felt together. Sew around the sewing line, leaving an opening for stuffing.

4. Draw on arms and legs.

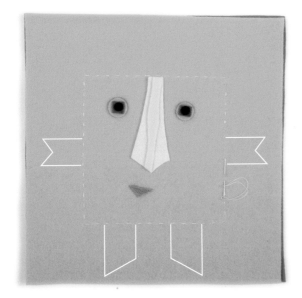

5

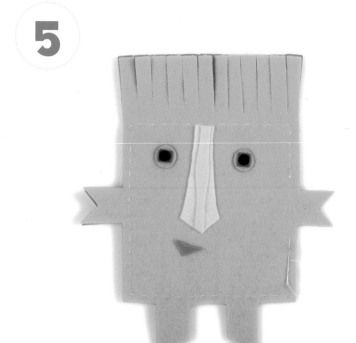

5. Cut around the arms and legs. Fringe the felt on the head where you want hair. Remember to cut at least 0.25" from the sewing line.

6. Stuff and sew the opening closed.

7. Cut off the top or bottom layer of felt from the arms, legs, or hair for different effects.

6

CiRCLe ZeNKi

What You Need in Addition to Your Basic Kit

• Two different-colored 9" × 9" squares of felt
• Felt for facial features

When I was younger, I'm talking in my twenties, I taught Hebrew to primary school children. I made up three characters that I loved to use in my lessons: Mr. Ribooa (Mr. Square), Mr. Igool (Mr. Circle), and Mrs. Mshoolash (Mrs. Triangle). I had so much fun with these three. They had very different personalities and were always getting into all sorts of mischief. After I'd made Square Zenki, I knew it was only a matter of time before Circle Zenki and Triangle Zenki would turn up on my doorstep.

How to Make Circle Zenki

1. Draw a circle with a 5″ diameter in the center of one of your 9″ × 9″ felt squares. This will be your sewing line.

2. Cut out facial features from felt. Position and glue into place.

3. Pin the two squares of felt together. Sew around the sewing line, leaving an opening for stuffing.

4. Draw on arms and legs.

5. Cut around the arms and legs. Fringe the felt on the head where you want hair. Remember to cut at least 0.25″ from the sewing line.

6. Stuff and sew the opening closed.

7. Cut off the top or bottom layer of felt from the arms, legs, or hair for different effects.

TRIANGLE ZENKI

What You Need in Addition to Your Basic Kit

- Two different-colored 9" × 9" squares of felt
- Felt for facial features

Triangle Zenki is the third in my trio. You might have noticed that he's not a pure triangle. He doesn't have a pointy head. That's because a point doesn't leave much room for brains. And

Triangle Zenki is a thinker. He works things out. He looks before he leaps. A pointy head doesn't leave much room for hair either. And Triangle Zenki likes to look sharp.

How to Make Triangle Zenki

1. Draw a triangle with a 7" base in the center of one of the 9" × 9" felt squares. The line of the triangle will be your sewing line. Note that the top of my triangle is flat rather than pointy.

2. Cut out facial features from felt. Position and glue into place. I've used a crossstitch to hold the eyes in place and used pinking shears to create his mouth.

3. Pin the two squares of felt together. Sew around the sewing line, leaving an opening for stuffing.

4 DRAW ON ARMS AND LEGS.

5

CUT AROUND THE ARMS AND LEGS. FRINGE THE FELT ON THE HEAD WHERE YOU WANT HAIR. REMEMBER TO CUT AT LEAST 0.25" FROM THE SEWING LINE.

6

STUFF AND SEW THE OPENING CLOSED.

7 CUT OFF THE TOP OR BOTTOM LAYER OF FELT FROM THE ARMS, LEGS, OR HAIR FOR DIFFERENT EFFECTS.

"HE IS SO CUTE THAT WHEN
I LOOK AT HIM MY HEART
JUST MELTS."

—JILLIAN, 11,
PATTERN TESTER

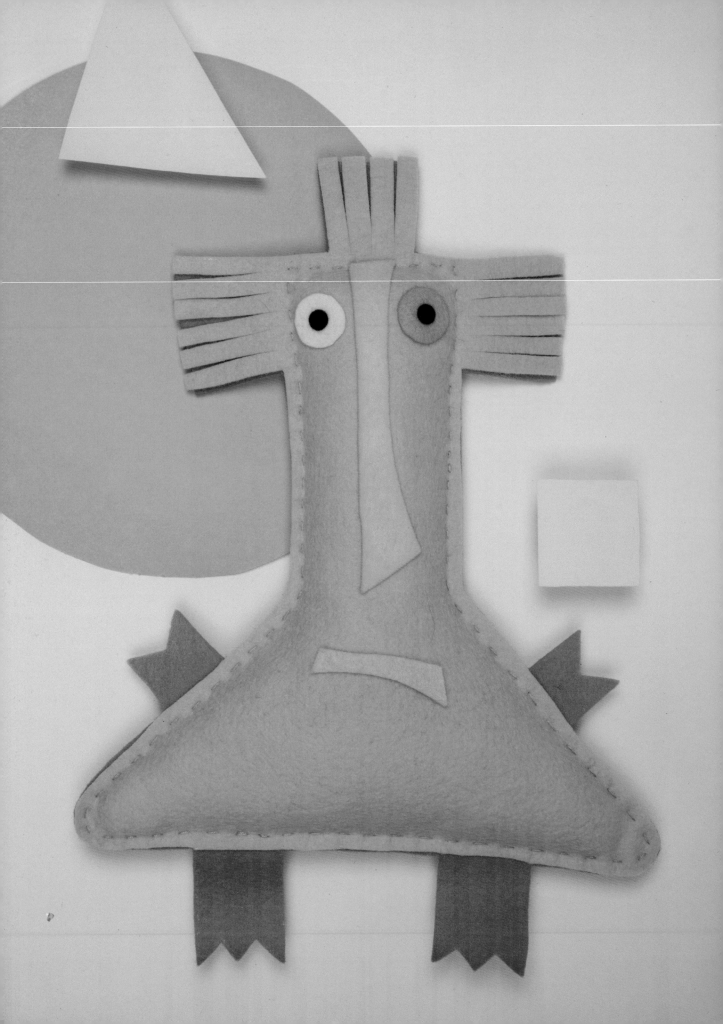

MIXED-UP ZENKI

What You Need in Addition to Your Basic Kit

- Two different-colored 9″ × 12″ pieces of felt
- Felt for facial features

I have a question: What happens when all these zenkis, these square and circle and triangle people, start mixing and matching? Well, we get Mixed-Up Zenkis. Not that the zenkis are mixed up or confused. They just become an engaging mix of different shapes and personalities. A Mixed-Up Zenki is a call to imagine for yourself completely new geometrical shapes by mixing and matching more-predictable ones. Mixed-Up Zenkis love to take that all-important step from the known to the unknown. And they want you to take it with them.

1 USE YOUR IMAGINATION TO DRAW A BODY SHAPE ONTO ONE OF THE 9" × 12" PIECES OF FELT. AS ALWAYS, THE LINE YOU DRAW WILL BE YOUR SEWING LINE.

2 CUT OUT FACIAL FEATURES FROM FELT. POSITION AND GLUE INTO PLACE.

3 PIN THE TWO SQUARES OF FELT TOGETHER. SEW AROUND THE SEWING LINE, LEAVING AN OPENING FOR STUFFING.

4 DRAW ON ARMS AND LEGS.

5 CUT AROUND THE ARMS AND LEGS. FRINGE THE FELT ON THE HEAD WHERE YOU WANT HAIR. REMEMBER TO CUT AT LEAST 0.25" FROM THE SEWING LINE.

6 STUFF AND SEW THE OPENING CLOSED.

7 CUT OFF THE TOP OR BOTTOM LAYER OF FELT FROM THE ARMS, LEGS, OR HAIR FOR DIFFERENT EFFECTS.

EVOLVING YOUR ZENKIS

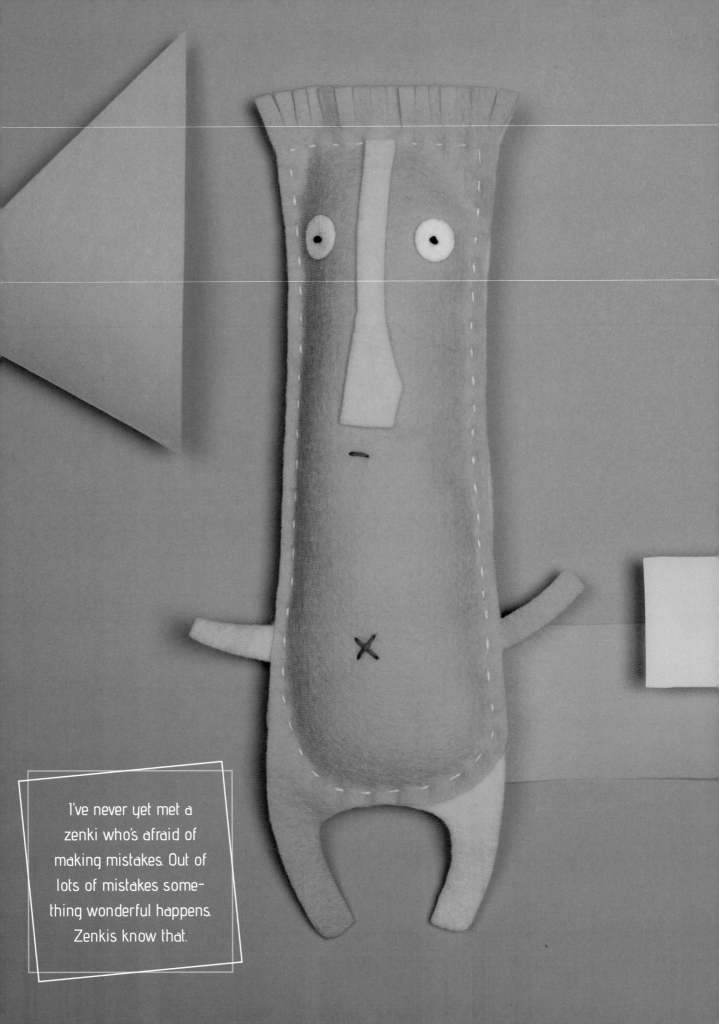

I've never yet met a zenki who's afraid of making mistakes. Out of lots of mistakes something wonderful happens. Zenkis know that.

LONG TALL ZENKi

What You Need in Addition to Your Basic Kit

- 11" × 7" light-green felt
- 11" × 7" light-yellow felt
- Yellow and white felt for eyes and nose

Now that you've learned how to sew zenkis from simple geometrical shapes, you can experiment with other kinds of shapes. This greatly increases the number of zenkis you can create. Long Tall Zenki is a good example of this group. She still looks a little like her more geometrical cousins, but truth is, she's the beginning of a whole new world of zenki possibilities. Originally she was designed as a flat bookmark and called Long Tall Sally, but as soon as I saw her, I knew she'd be a wonderful zenki.

1

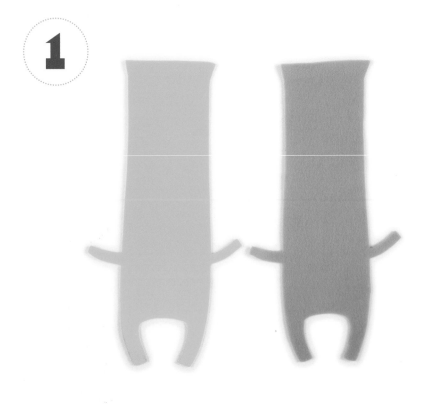

2

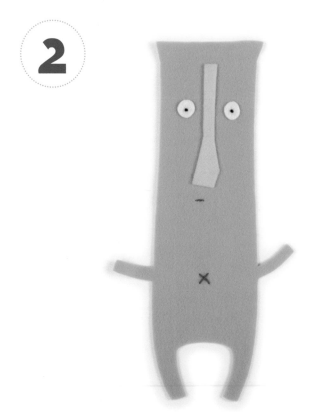

1. Copy and cut out the template. Trace the template onto the two 11" × 7" pieces of felt and cut out.

2. Cut out facial features and glue or sew into place. I chose to sew on the eyes by using a French knot for the pupil. If you glue on the eyes, you can make the pupil by placing the lead point of a 2B or 3B pencil in the center of the eye and turning it around without moving the pencil from its place. I used a single red stitch to make a mouth and a red cross stitch for the belly button. I glued the nose into place.

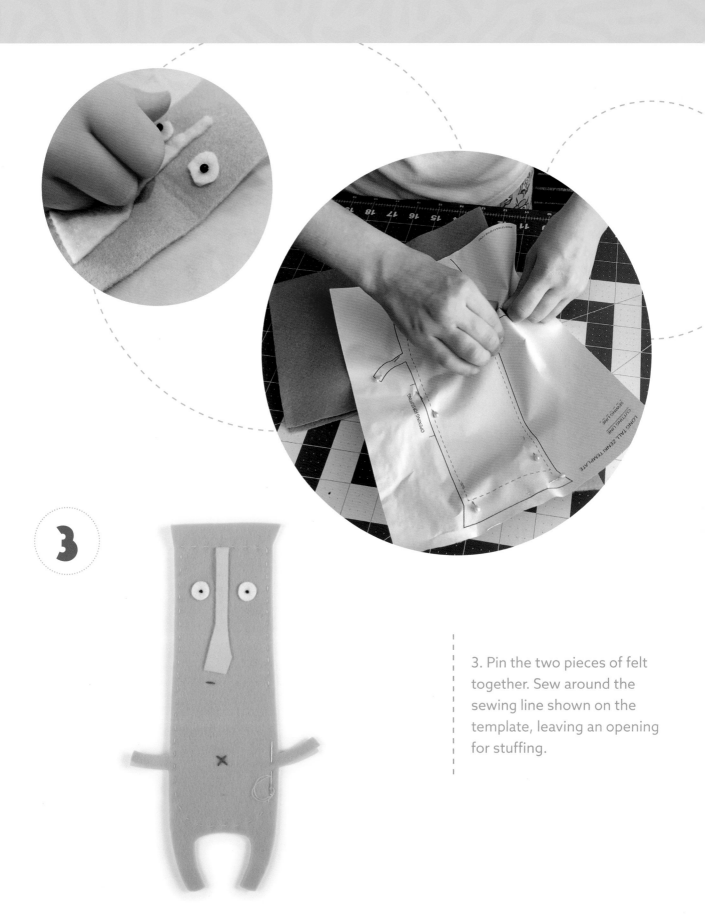

3

3. Pin the two pieces of felt together. Sew around the sewing line shown on the template, leaving an opening for stuffing.

4

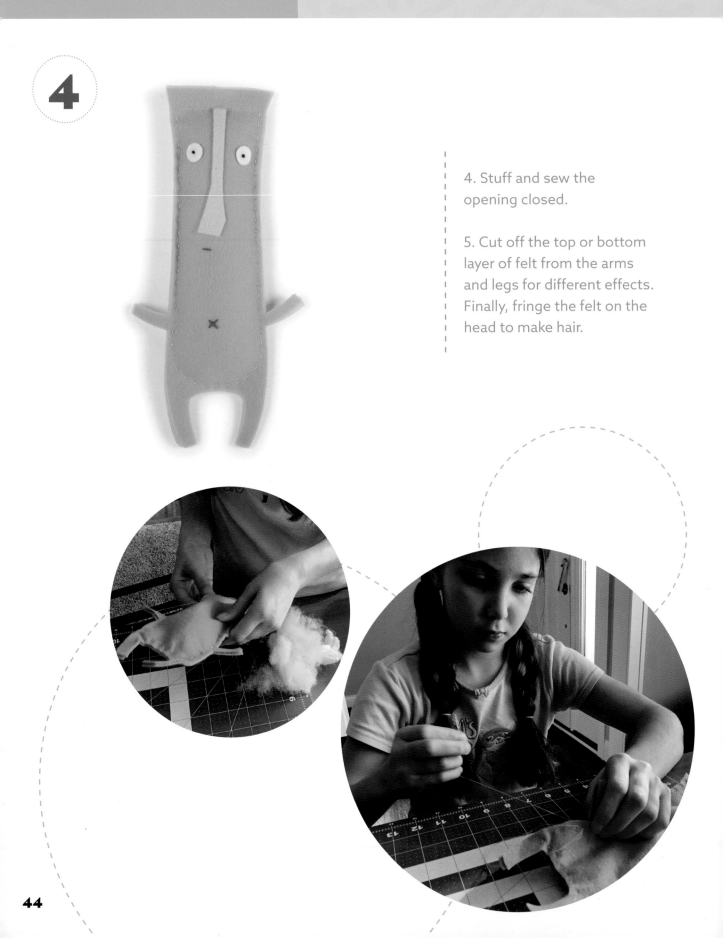

4. Stuff and sew the opening closed.

5. Cut off the top or bottom layer of felt from the arms and legs for different effects. Finally, fringe the felt on the head to make hair.

5

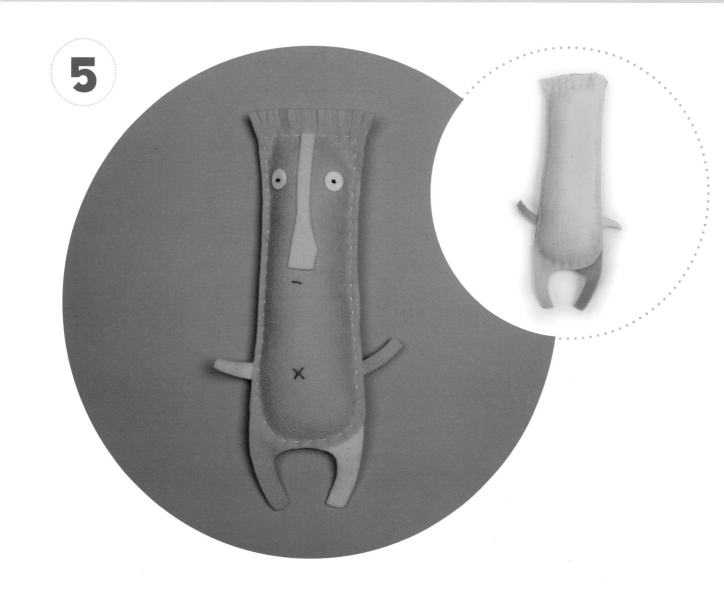

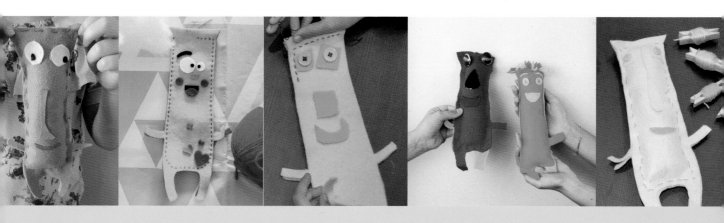

NOTE TO FUTURE MINI MONSTER OWNERS

When you make mini monsters, you can have fun creating a whole crowd of them. They like this immensely because then they have lots of friends. A really simple way to give your mini monsters a unique personality is to vary one of their features. You can see that I've chosen to vary their ears. Mini monsters are a wild, lively lot, and they love their ears and listening to everything that's going on around them.

MiNi MONSTER

- 5" × 4" green felt
- 5" × 4" dark-yellow felt
- White felt for facial features

I want to tell you a true story about mini monsters. This happened a few years ago in Florida, USA. A Sew a Softie participant knew a three-year-old boy who was too afraid to play on his local jungle gym. Apparently, an older boy had told him that monsters lived there. What did she do? She made some of these mini monsters, gave them to him, and told him that his little monster friends would protect him from any other monsters living in the jungle gym. From that day on, he wasn't afraid to play there. Mini monsters might be little, but they can make a really big difference.

TIP FOR PARENTS
One way to help kids make their own monsters is to draw a simple peanut-shaped body onto paper and let your kids add whatever kinds of hands, feet, ears, horns, spikes, etc. that they want. Cut out their drawing, copy it onto your felt, and make it into a zenki.

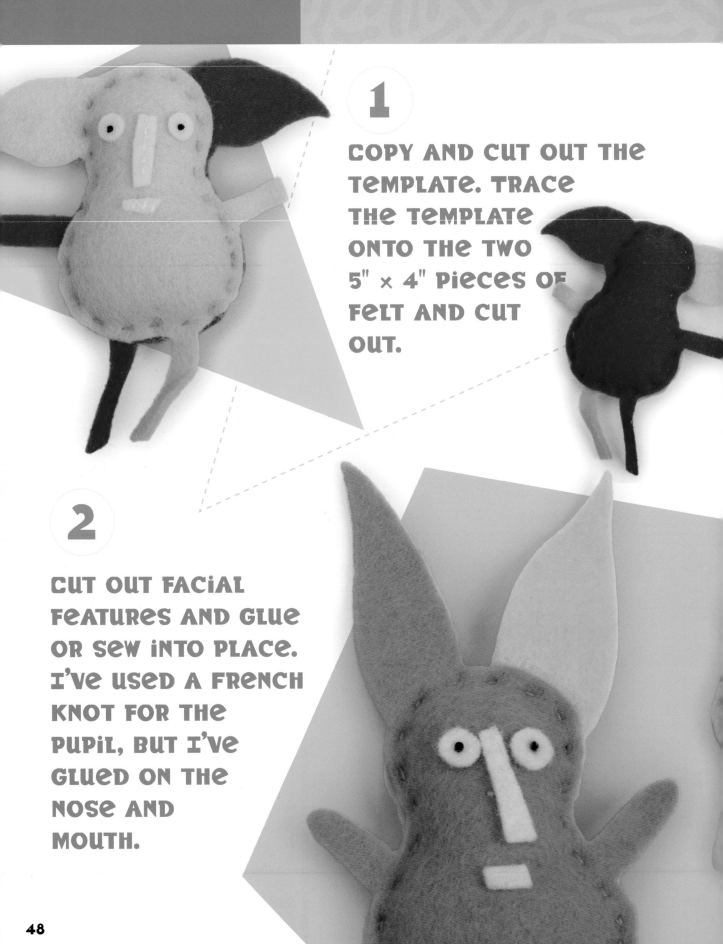

1

COPY AND CUT OUT THE TEMPLATE. TRACE THE TEMPLATE ONTO THE TWO 5" × 4" PIECES OF FELT AND CUT OUT.

2

CUT OUT FACIAL FEATURES AND GLUE OR SEW INTO PLACE. I'VE USED A FRENCH KNOT FOR THE PUPIL, BUT I'VE GLUED ON THE NOSE AND MOUTH.

3 PIN THE TWO PIECES OF FELT TOGETHER. SEW AROUND THE SEWING LINE SHOWN ON THE TEMPLATE, LEAVING AN OPENING FOR STUFFING.

4 STUFF AND SEW THE OPENING CLOSED.

5 CUT OFF THE TOP OR BOTTOM LAYER OF FELT FROM THE EARS, ARMS, AND LEGS FOR DIFFERENT EFFECTS.

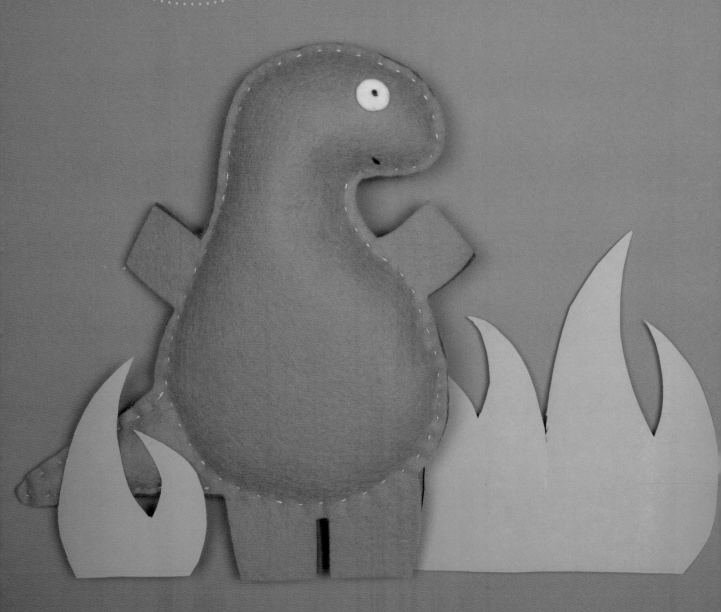

NOTE ON
JOSHUASAURUS

My Joshuasaurus is lighter on one
side than on the other, as though sun-
light is shining on one side of him. This
means that his arms and legs have two
layers of felt. You can leave these two
layers just as they are, as I have done,
or you can stick them together
with a drop of glue.

JOSHUA SAURUS

What You Need in Addition to Your Basic Kit

• 10" × 10" dark-brown felt
• 10" × 10" light-brown felt
• White felt for eyes

I have a good friend who lives in Paris. It's surprising that we get on so well, since she doesn't speak much English and I don't speak much French. She has a six-year-old grandson named Joshua, who often sends me things. One day Joshua sent me his drawing of a dinosaur. He loves dinosaurs. It was a very sweet drawing, and I decided I'd make a dinosaur zenki that was something like his drawing, and send it back to him. In his honor, I called my dinosaur Joshuasaurus.

1 COPY AND CUT OUT THE TEMPLATE. TRACE THE TEMPLATE ONTO THE TWO 10" × 10" PIECES OF FELT AND CUT OUT.

2 CUT OUT EYES AND GLUE OR SEW INTO PLACE.

I've cut out two 0.5" diameter circles for the eyes from white felt. I've made an eye for each side of the head and sewn each eye into place, using a French knot for the pupil. I've used a single stitch of black thread to make a smiling mouth. Joshuasaurus is a happy fellow. Nothing gets him down.

3 PIN THE TWO PIECES OF FELT TOGETHER. SEW AROUND HIS BODY ON THE SEWING LINE MARKED ON THE TEMPLATE, LEAVING AN OPENING FOR STUFFING.

4 STUFF AND SEW THE BODY CLOSED.

5 SEW AROUND THE TAIL, LEAVING AN OPENING FOR STUFFING.

6 STUFF AND SEW THE OPENING CLOSED. ALTERNATIVELY, LEAVE THE TAIL UNSEWN.

MARViN

55

What You Need in Addition to Your Basic Kit

- 8" × 8" red felt
- 8" × 8" blue felt
- 5" × 5" white felt for mouth
- White and black felt for eyes
- Rice for weighting

I've traveled all over the world with Marvin . . . actually, with the whole Marvin family. Great travelers. They loved Paris, the Louvre, and street graffiti wherever it was. Marvin is something of a street-graffiti connoisseur—but it has to be creative, lively, colorful . . . it has to brighten life up to win Marvin's approval.

Marvin has been around, he's seen the world, and he lives life to the full. He lives its ups and its downs. He has his good days and his bad days. I have to say, he can be trying at times, but I love traveling with him. Life is never boring when Marvin is around.

1 COPY AND CUT OUT THE TEMPLATES. TRACE THE BODY TEMPLATE ONTO THE 8" × 8" PIECES OF FELT AND CUT OUT. TRACE THE MOUTH TEMPLATE ONTO THE 5" × 5" WHITE FELT AND CUT OUT TWO MOUTHS, ONE FOR EACH SIDE OF MARVIN.

2 TO MAKE THE EYES, CUT OUT TWO 1" DIAMETER CIRCLES. FOR THE PUPIL, I'VE USED A HOLE PUNCH TO PUNCH OUT A SMALL CIRCLE OF BLACK FELT.

3 PIN AND SEW THE MOUTHS INTO PLACE. USE THE SEWING LINE INDICATED ON THE MOUTH TEMPLATE. REMEMBER, ON ONE SIDE HE HAS A SMILING MOUTH, AND ON HIS OTHER SIDE, A FROWNING ONE.

4 GLUE THE PUPILS ONTO THE 1" CIRCLES OF WHITE FELT, THEN SEW OR GLUE THE EYES INTO PLACE.

5 PIN AND SEW THE TWO SIDES OF MARVIN TOGETHER, LEAVING AN OPENING FOR STUFFING.

6 FILL THE BOTTOM THIRD OF MARVIN WITH RICE GRAINS. STUFF THE REMAINDER AND SEW THE OPENING CLOSED.

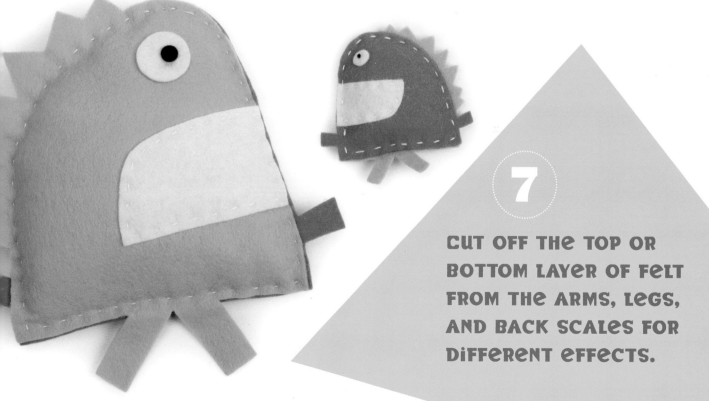

7 CUT OFF THE TOP OR BOTTOM LAYER OF FELT FROM THE ARMS, LEGS, AND BACK SCALES FOR DIFFERENT EFFECTS.

TIP ON FRINGING

An easy way to make your fringes more or less the same is to make your first cut in the middle of the fin or tail, dividing it into two sections. Then cut each of those sections in their middle and so on. Also, be careful not to make the fringes too thin, since they might break off at their base. You might also have noticed that for the tail, I made only three cuts because I thought it made the tail look a bit sturdier and more tail-like.

NOTE ON SETH'S EYE

My Seth has an eye on one side only, but you can also give your Seth an eye and side fin on his other side if you wish. Both ways work.

SETH

59

What You Need in Addition to Your Basic Kit

- 10" × 10" orange felt
- 10" × 10" blue felt
- White felt for eye
- Button for pupil of eye

I'm a Bondi girl. I don't know if you've heard of Bondi Beach, but it's pretty famous. Probably Australia's best-known beach. Living by the beach, I love to swim. I sometimes wonder what it would be like to be a fish in the sea. You'd want big eyes to see everything down there. And to avoid the sharks.

One day, Seth swam into view. I can't tell you exactly where he came from, because fish sort of just appear from nowhere and vanish again.

I *can* tell you that Bondi gets pretty hot in the summer, but no matter how hot it gets, Seth is always going to be the coolest guy in town.

1 COPY AND CUT OUT THE TEMPLATES. TRACE THE BODY TEMPLATE ONTO THE 10" × 10" PIECES OF FELT AND CUT OUT. TRACE THE SIDE-FIN TEMPLATE ONTO ORANGE FELT AND CUT OUT.

2 TO MAKE THE EYE, CUT OUT A 2" DIAMETER CIRCLE FROM WHITE FELT. SEW ON A BUTTON FOR THE PUPIL. ALTERNATIVELY, YOU CAN GLUE ON A PUPIL. SEW THE COMPLETED EYE INTO PLACE, LEAVING AN OPENING FOR STUFFING. PUSH A LITTLE STUFFING INTO THE EYE AND SEW THE OPENING CLOSED.

3 PIN AND SEW THE SIDE FIN INTO PLACE. ALTERNATIVELY, GLUE IT ON.

4 PIN THE TWO SIDES OF SETH TOGETHER.

5 DRAW THE CURVED LINE FOR SETH'S MOUTH ONTO THE FELT. TO SEW THE TWO SIDES OF SETH TOGETHER, START SEWING FROM THE MOUTH. CONTINUE TO SEW AROUND THE BOTTOM OF SETH'S BODY TILL YOU GET ABOUT HALFWAY ALONG. AT THIS POINT, IT'S A GOOD IDEA TO STUFF THE AREA UNDER SETH'S MOUTH. CONTINUE SEWING AROUND THE BODY BUT LEAVE AN OPENING FOR STUFFING, AS INDICATED ON THE TEMPLATE.

6 STUFF THE REMAINDER OF SETH'S BODY AND SEW THE OPENING CLOSED.

7 FRINGE THE TOP, SIDE, AND BOTTOM FINS AND THE TAIL. CUT OFF THE TOP OR BOTTOM LAYER OF FELT FROM THE FINS AND TAIL FOR DIFFERENT EFFECTS.

THE SKY'S THE LIMIT

TREE FROGGY

What You Need in Addition to Your Basic Kit

- 10" × 8" orange felt
- 5" × 5" aqua felt
- White and black felt for eyes
- Felt for mouth
- Rice for weighting

Using the same front and back shape for your zenki makes lots of sense, but it's not always going to be the most effective method of designing. There will be times where it's simpler, and more logical, to make your zenki from two different shapes. This chapter explores the kind of zenkis you can design when the front and back shapes are no longer the same.

Tree Froggy is the first example of this group of zenkis. Please put your hands together for him so we can get on with this . . . he's a born performer and just soaks up applause.

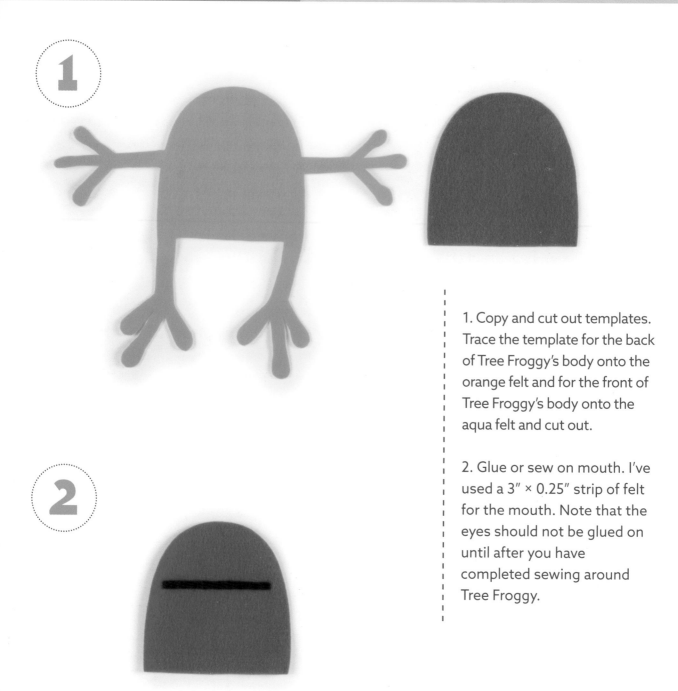

1

2

1. Copy and cut out templates. Trace the template for the back of Tree Froggy's body onto the orange felt and for the front of Tree Froggy's body onto the aqua felt and cut out.

2. Glue or sew on mouth. I've used a 3" × 0.25" strip of felt for the mouth. Note that the eyes should not be glued on until after you have completed sewing around Tree Froggy.

3

4

3. Pin the front and back of Tree Froggy's body together. Sew around the sewing line as indicated on the template, leaving an opening for stuffing at the top of his head.

4. Fill the bottom half of Tree Froggy with rice grains. Stuff the top half and sew the opening closed.

5

5. Glue Tree Froggy's eyes into place. I've used a 0.75" diameter white felt circle for the eyes and punched out black felt circles for the pupils.

BETTY BAT

What You Need in Addition to Your Basic Kit

- 14" × 12" magenta felt
- 12" × 10" dark pink felt
- Felt for facial features

Outside my bedroom window, a huge mulberry tree grows. When the mulberries are ripe, fruit bats fly in almost every night. They make the cutest sounds. It was a good bet that one day, I'd make a bat zenki. Originally her name wasn't Betty. I called her Batty bat. Not very imaginative, I know, but it did have a distinctive ring.

Soon after I made her, I took her along to a little Italian café near where I live called La Piadina. Damiano, the owner, is a friend. As I walked in, he asked me what I was holding. "This is Batty bat," I said. Amusingly, Damiano sometimes mishears my vowels and replied, "Oh, Betty bat; I like her." And that's how Betty got her name.

1 COPY AND CUT OUT TEMPLATES. TRACE THE TEMPLATE FOR THE BACK OF BETTY'S BODY ONTO THE MAGENTA FELT AND FOR THE FRONT OF HER BODY ONTO THE DARK PINK FELT AND CUT OUT.

2 GLUE OR SEW ON FACIAL FEATURES.

3 PIN THE FRONT AND BACK OF BETTY'S BODY TOGETHER. SEW AROUND THE SEWING LINE AS INDICATED ON THE TEMPLATE, LEAVING AN OPENING FOR STUFFING.

4 STUFF AND SEW THE OPENING CLOSED.

5 ATTACH THE END OF EACH ARM TO ITS WING WITH A DROP OF GLUE.

GWENNiE UNiCORN

What You Need in Addition to Your Basic Kit

- 14" × 10" green felt
- 10" × 7" pink felt
- Golden-yellow felt for hooves and horn
- Black and white felt for eyes
- Rice for weighting

Kids, especially girls, are fascinated by unicorns. My own interest in unicorns was piqued when I got the opportunity to hold a unicorn-sewing workshop in conjunction with the Lady and the Unicorn tapestries, which were being exhibited at the Art Gallery of New South Wales in Sydney. The unicorn I designed for that workshop was fairly straightforward, with rich decorative additions and shiny rhinestones. My Gwennie has less sparkle but more flair. She's the sort of unicorn you might find living next door. And she has a bit of attitude. She's also nothing like the unicorn in those medieval tapestries . . . but she's every bit as magical.

1 COPY AND CUT OUT THE TEMPLATES. TRACE THE TEMPLATE FOR THE BACK OF GWENNIE'S BODY ONTO THE GREEN FELT, FOR THE FRONT OF HER BODY ONTO THE PINK FELT, AND FOR HER HOOVES AND HORN ONTO GOLDEN-YELLOW FELT AND CUT OUT.

2 GLUE OR SEW ON HER EYE.

3 I'VE CUT OUT A 0.75" DIAMETER CIRCLE FOR HER EYE FROM WHITE FELT AND PUNCHED OUT A BLACK FELT CIRCLE FOR THE PUPIL AND GLUED THEM ON.

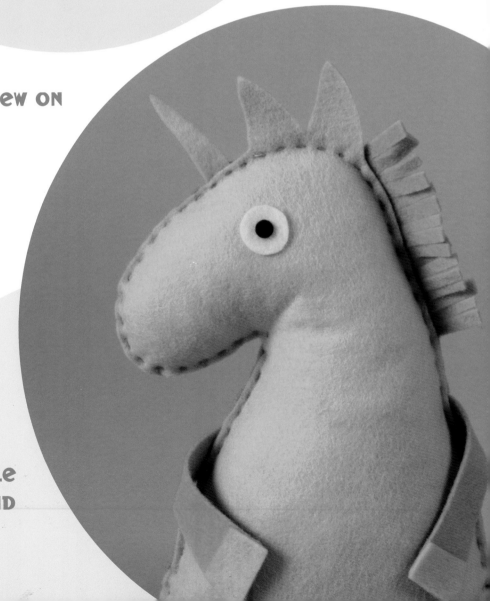

4

PIN THE FRONT AND BACK OF GWENNIE'S BODY TOGETHER. PIN HER HORN INTO PLACE BY INSERTING IT BETWEEN THE FRONT AND BACK LAYERS OF FELT. SEW AROUND THE SEWING LINE AS INDICATED ON THE TEMPLATE, LEAVING AN OPENING FOR STUFFING AT THE TOP OF HER HEAD.

5 FILL THE BOTTOM THIRD OF GWENNIE WITH RICE GRAINS. STUFF AND SEW THE OPENING CLOSED.

6 FRINGE GWENNIE'S MANE AND GLUE HER HOOVES INTO PLACE.

LiTTLe FOX

What You Need in Addition to Your Basic Kit

• 12" × 12" brown felt
• 10" × 10" white felt
• Black felt for eyes and nose
• Dark-gray felt for mouth

I've heard that there are two kinds of people in this world: cat people and dog people. I don't believe that. Take foxes as an example. Foxes look a bit like dogs but feel a bit like cats. And if you like foxes, and I do, then you can't be just a cat person or a dog person; you're both. Like all foxes, Little Fox has a dash of catlike independence. I like that.

How to Make Little Fox

1. Copy and cut out the templates. Trace the templates for the back of Little Fox's body, for his face mask, and for his tail onto the brown felt and cut out. Trace the templates for the front of his body, for the insides of his ears, and for his tail tip onto the white felt and cut out. Trace the template for his nose onto black felt and cut out.

2. Pin his face mask into place. Sew along the bottom of the mask as indicated on the template. Alternatively, glue the mask on.

3 GLUE ON HIS EYES, NOSE, AND MOUTH. I'VE PUNCHED OUT TWO BLACK FELT CIRCLES FOR THE EYES AND CUT A SMALL TRIANGLE OF DARK-GRAY FELT FOR HIS MOUTH.

4 PIN AND SEW THE INSIDES OF THE EARS INTO PLACE. ALTERNATIVELY, GLUE THEM ON.

5 PIN AND SEW THE WHITE TAIL TIP INTO PLACE. ALTERNATIVELY, GLUE IT ON.

6 PIN AND SEW HIS TAIL INTO PLACE.

7 NOW PIN THE FRONT AND BACK OF LITTLE FOX'S BODY TOGETHER AND SEW AROUND THE SEWING LINE AS INDICATED ON THE TEMPLATE, LEAVING AN OPENING FOR STUFFING.

8 STUFF AND SEW THE OPENING CLOSED.

"THE PATTERN IS EASY
TO FOLLOW AND I
UNDERSTOOD ALL THE
INSTRUCTIONS. I FOUND
IT EASY TO DESIGN MY
OWN CHARACTER. MY
NEXT ONE IS GOING TO
BE A FRENCH FRY!"

—HADASSAH, 11,
PATTERN TESTER

BELLA

What You Need in Addition to Your Basic Kit

- 13" × 8" yellow felt
- 10" × 6" orange felt
- Brown felt for facial features

Congratulations. Bella is our last project. By the time you've arrived at Bella, I'm hoping that you will be beginning to see a few things. I hope that you can still see Square Zenki in Bella. She does look different, that's true. But she's not. Not really. She still only requires you to sew around her body. Her arms, legs, whiskers, and the tuft of fur in the middle of her head are all still just cut from the margin. Only her nose is a smidgen more complex. And her swishy tail, that's also new. Square Zenki doesn't have one. He might wish he had one, but he doesn't. Not yet.

And I hope you can see how Bella is really just showing you the hidden potential that was always there in your very first zenki. Bella is a lioness, a mama, and always tells her cubs, "Just when you think you've arrived at the end of all you can do, you'll find something else, something new, waiting for you." Just as Bella was already waiting for us to find her in Square Zenki, I hope you can begin to see all the other unmade zenkis that are waiting to be found by us in Bella.

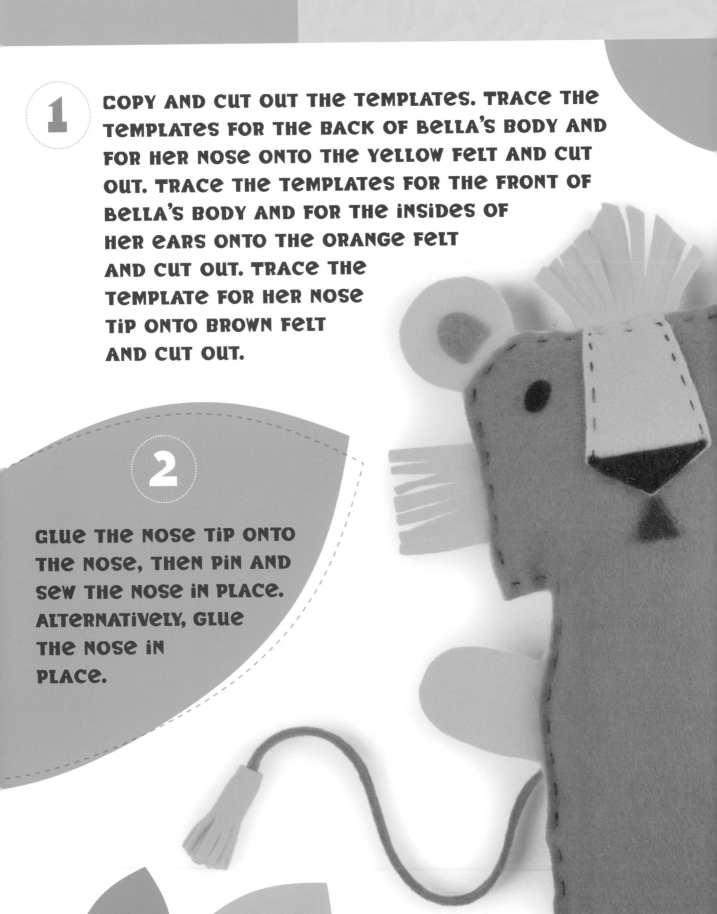

1 COPY AND CUT OUT THE TEMPLATES. TRACE THE TEMPLATES FOR THE BACK OF BELLA'S BODY AND FOR HER NOSE ONTO THE YELLOW FELT AND CUT OUT. TRACE THE TEMPLATES FOR THE FRONT OF BELLA'S BODY AND FOR THE INSIDES OF HER EARS ONTO THE ORANGE FELT AND CUT OUT. TRACE THE TEMPLATE FOR HER NOSE TIP ONTO BROWN FELT AND CUT OUT.

2 GLUE THE NOSE TIP ONTO THE NOSE, THEN PIN AND SEW THE NOSE IN PLACE. ALTERNATIVELY, GLUE THE NOSE IN PLACE.

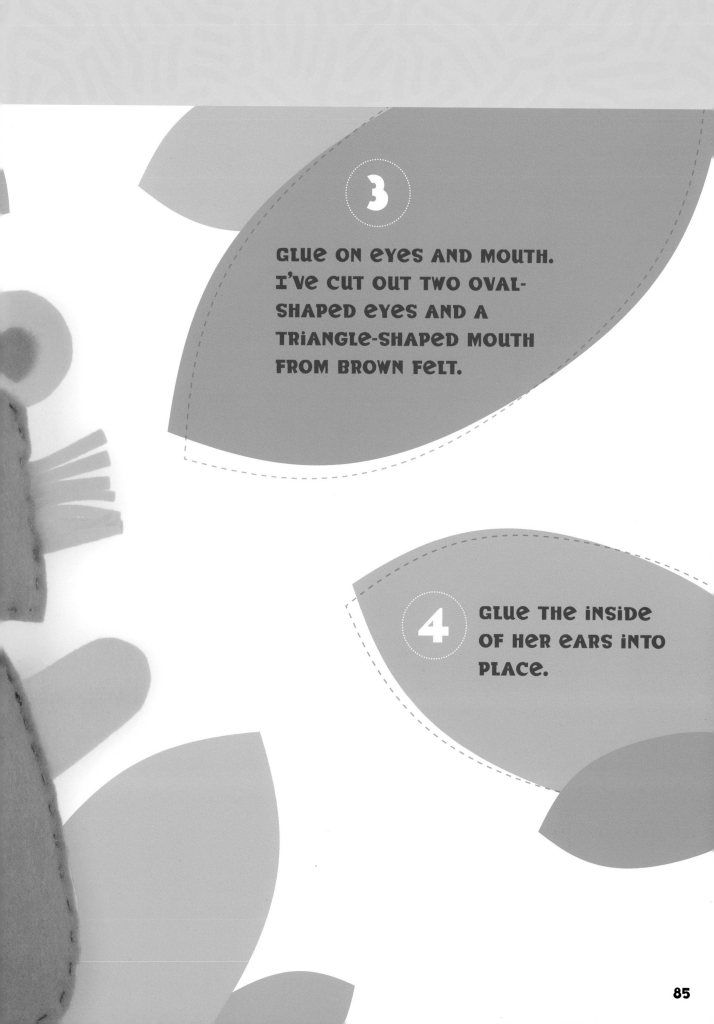

3

GLUE ON EYES AND MOUTH. I'VE CUT OUT TWO OVAL-SHAPED EYES AND A TRIANGLE-SHAPED MOUTH FROM BROWN FELT.

4 GLUE THE INSIDE OF HER EARS INTO PLACE.

5

TO MAKE BELLA'S TAIL, CUT A LONG, THIN STRIP OF ORANGE FELT AND A 3" × 1.25" RECTANGLE OF YELLOW FELT. FRINGE ONE SIDE OF THE RECTANGLE AND PUT SOME GLUE ALONG THE OPPOSITE, UNFRINGED SIDE. PLACE ONE END OF THE ORANGE STRIP ONTO THE UNFRINGED SIDE OF THE RECTANGLE AND ROLL THE RECTANGLE UP.

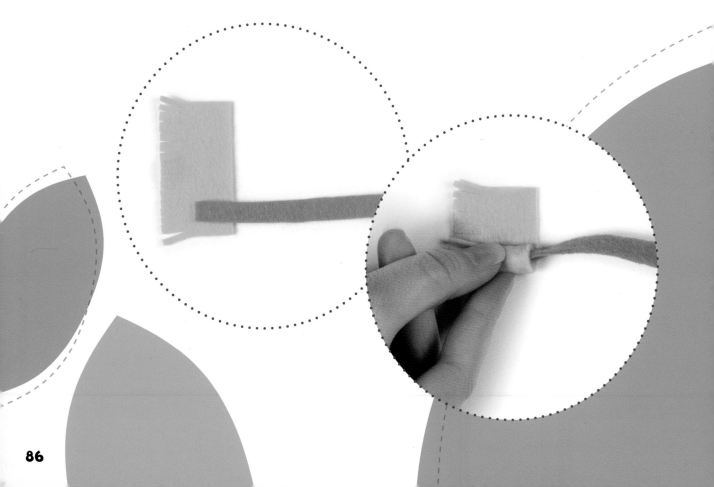

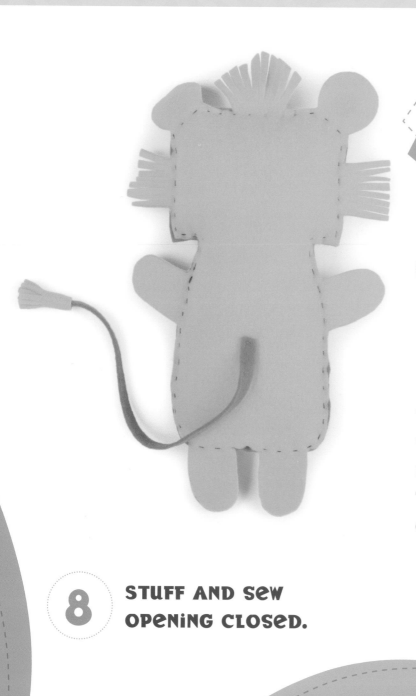

6

PIN AND SEW THE TAIL INTO PLACE.

7

PIN THE BACK AND FRONT OF BELLA'S BODY TOGETHER AND SEW AROUND THE SEWING LINE AS INDICATED ON THE TEMPLATE, LEAVING AN OPENING FOR STUFFING.

8 STUFF AND SEW OPENING CLOSED.

9 FRINGE THE TUFT OF HAIR ON BELLA'S HEAD AND HER WHISKERS.

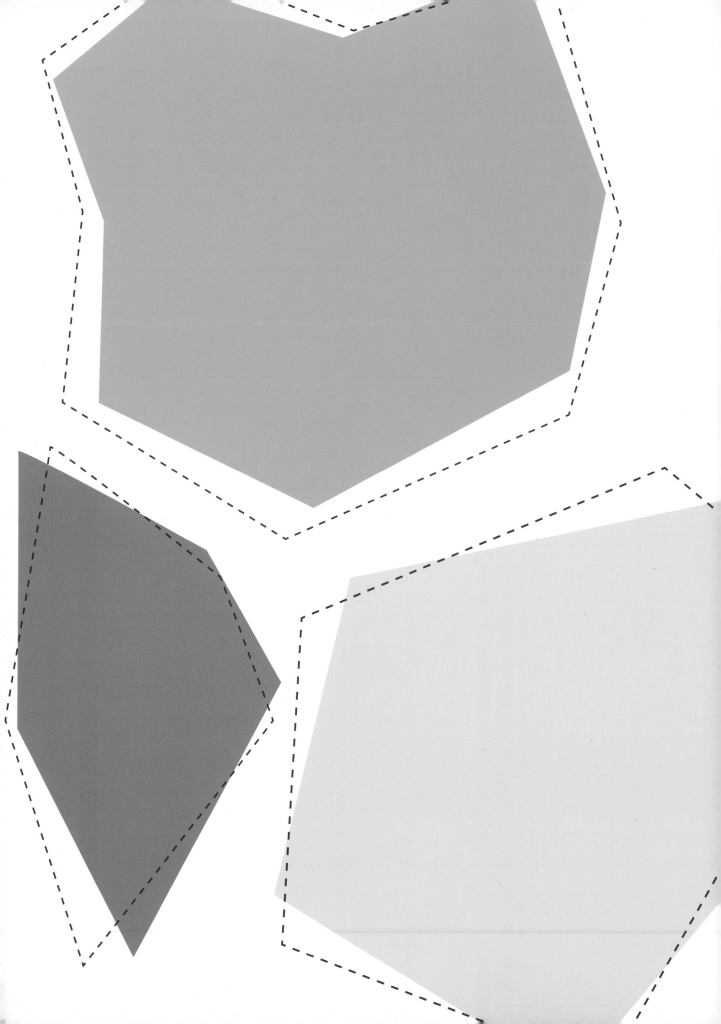

TEMPLATES

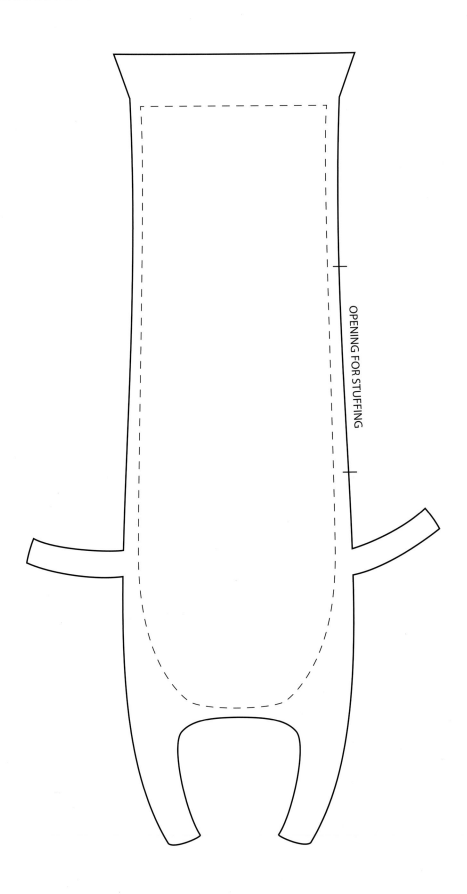

OPENING FOR STUFFING

OPENING FOR STUFFING

Joshuasaurus

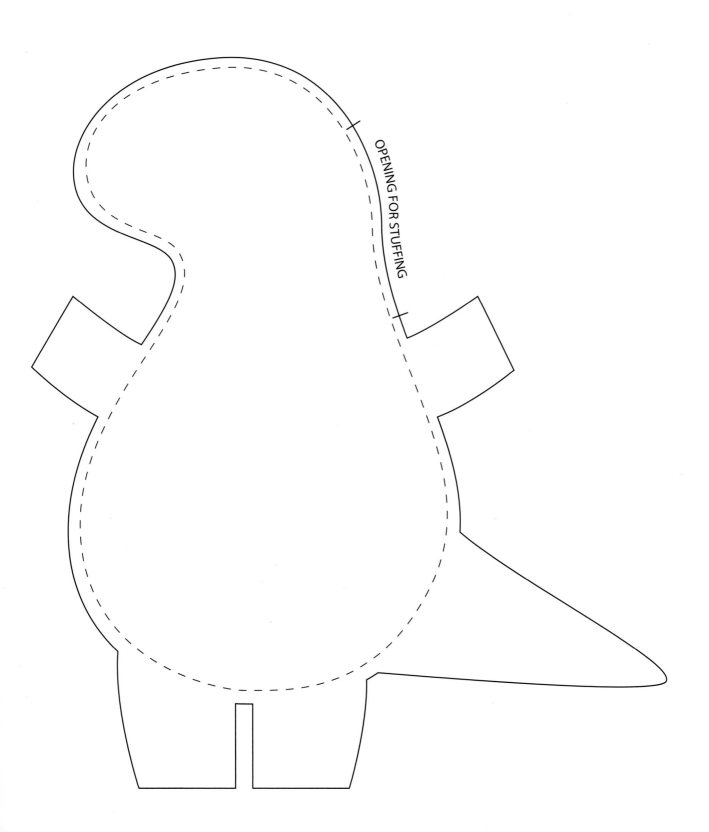

OPENING FOR STUFFING

Marvin

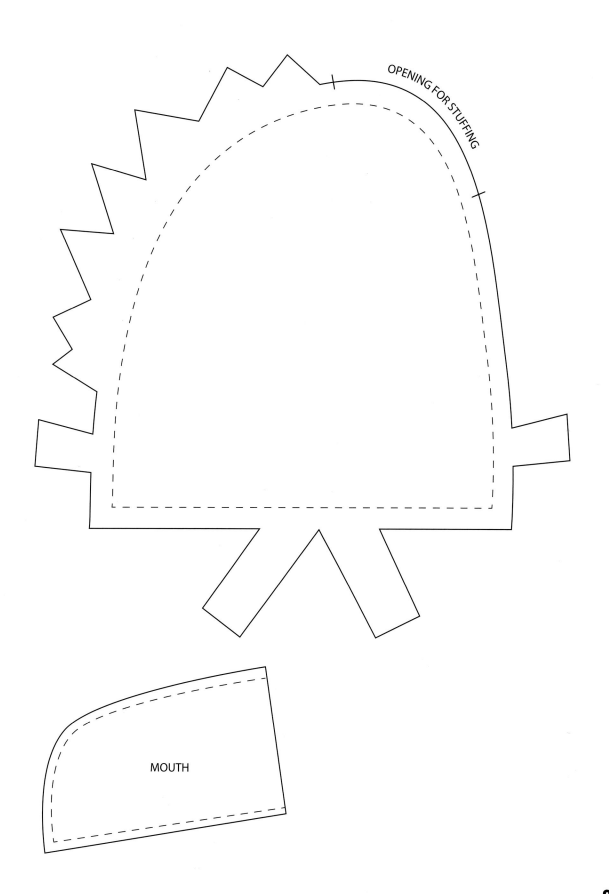

OPENING FOR STUFFING

MOUTH

Seth

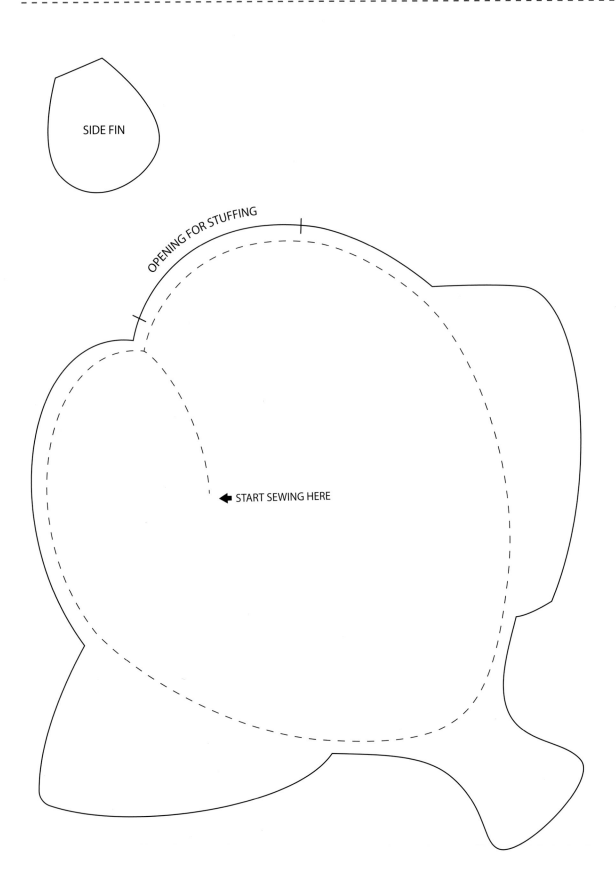

SIDE FIN

OPENING FOR STUFFING

◄ START SEWING HERE

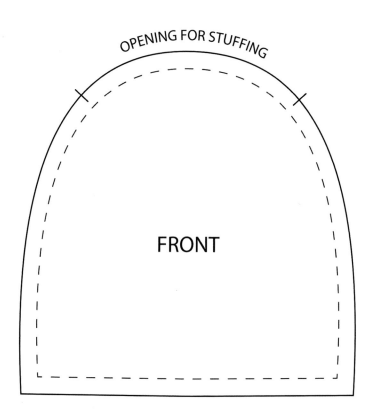

OPENING FOR STUFFING

FRONT

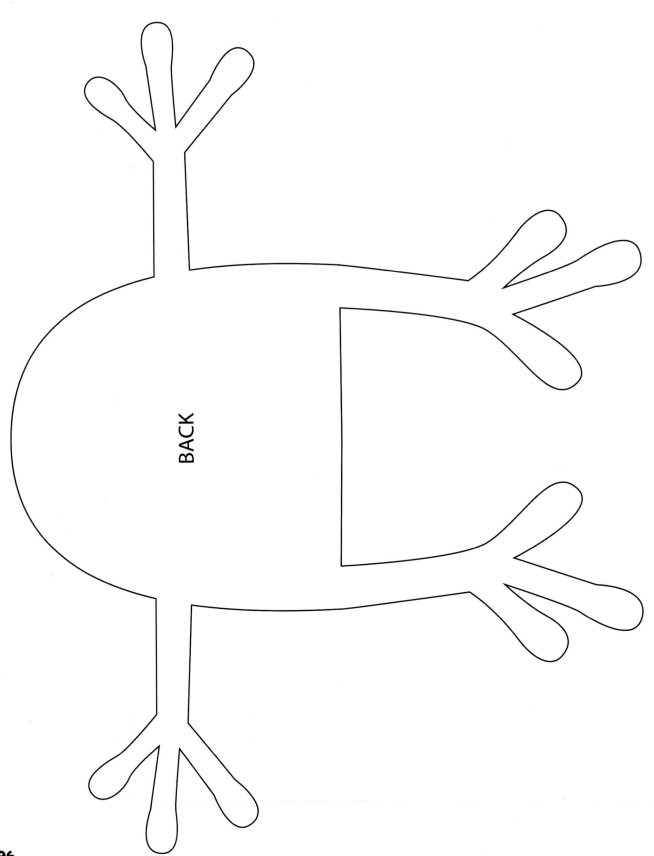

BACK

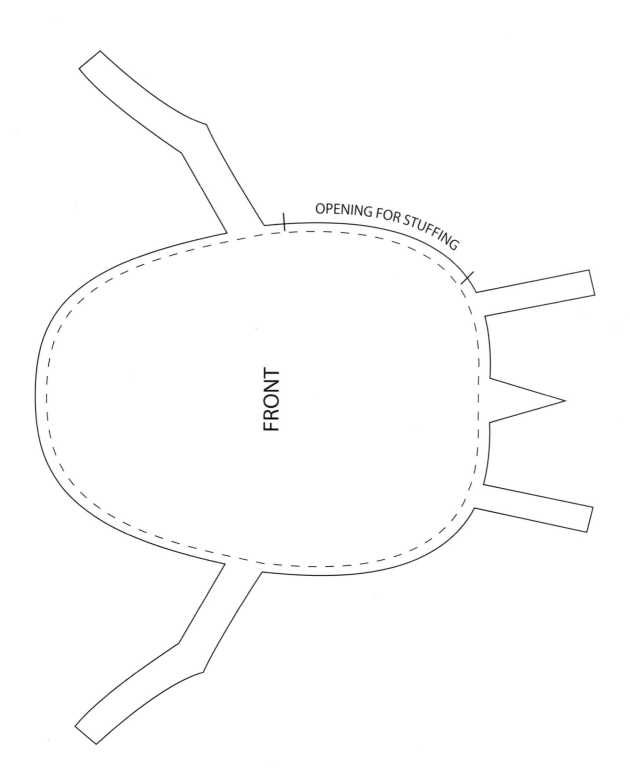

OPENING FOR STUFFING

FRONT

Betty Bat

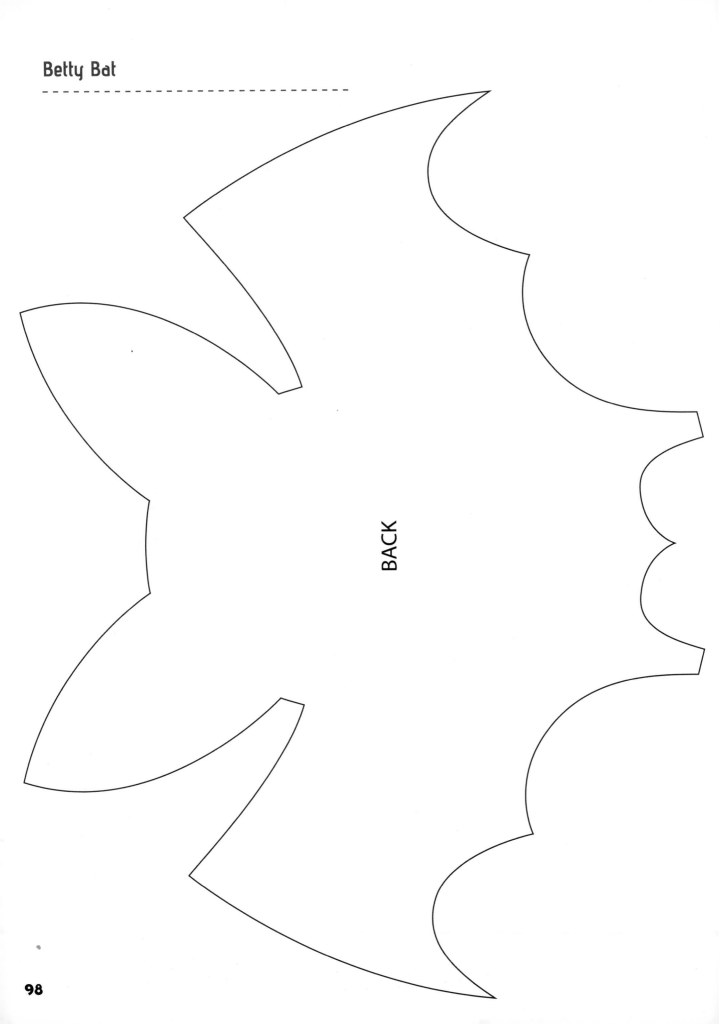

BACK

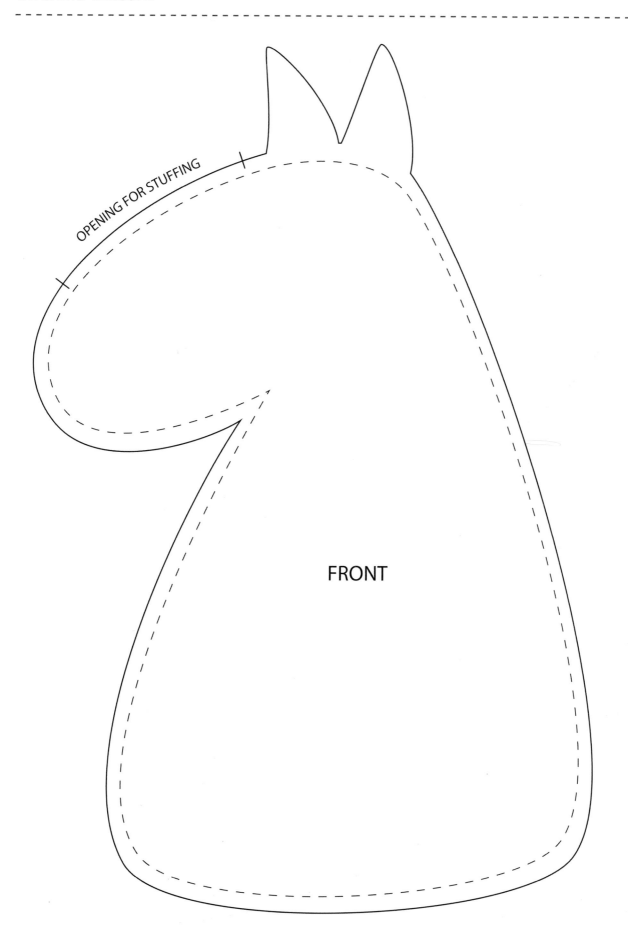

OPENING FOR STUFFING

FRONT

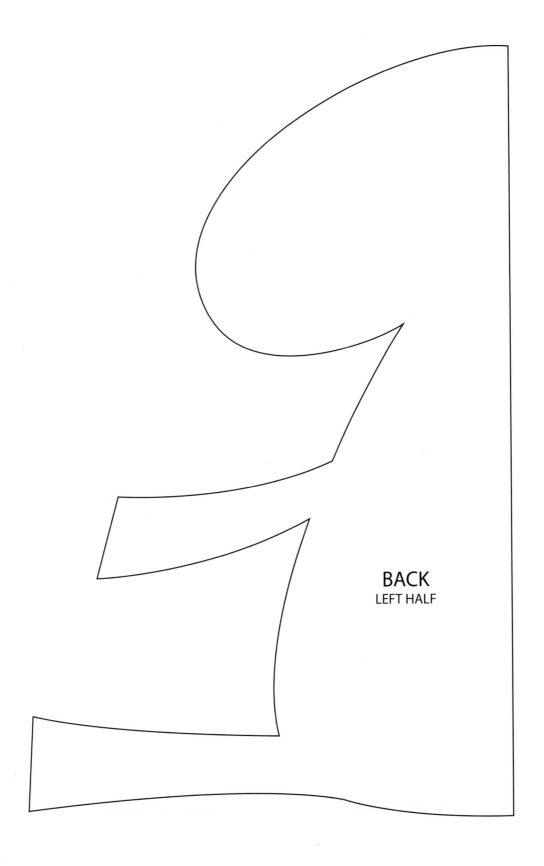

BACK
LEFT HALF

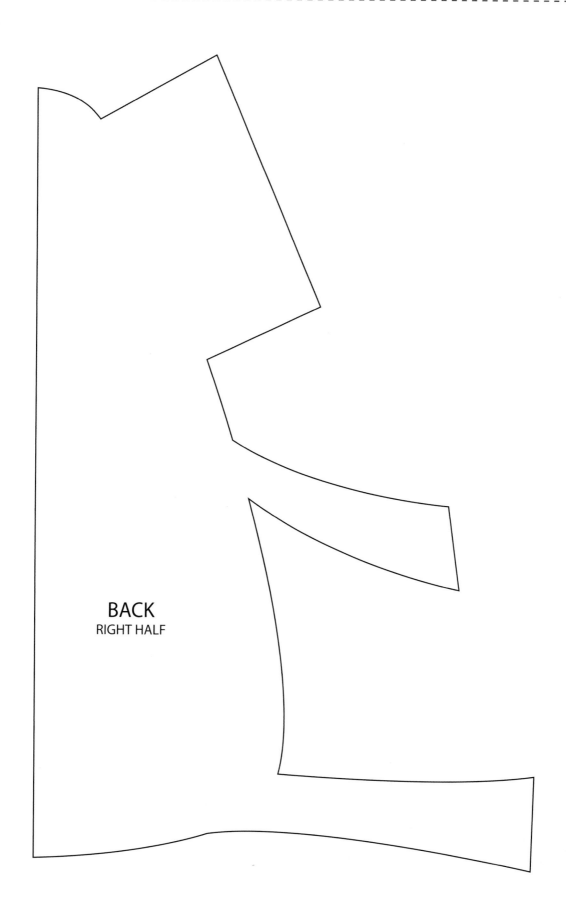

BACK
RIGHT HALF

HORN

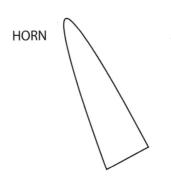

LEG HOOVES

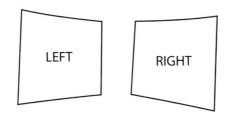

ARM HOOVES

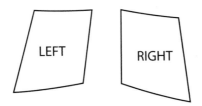

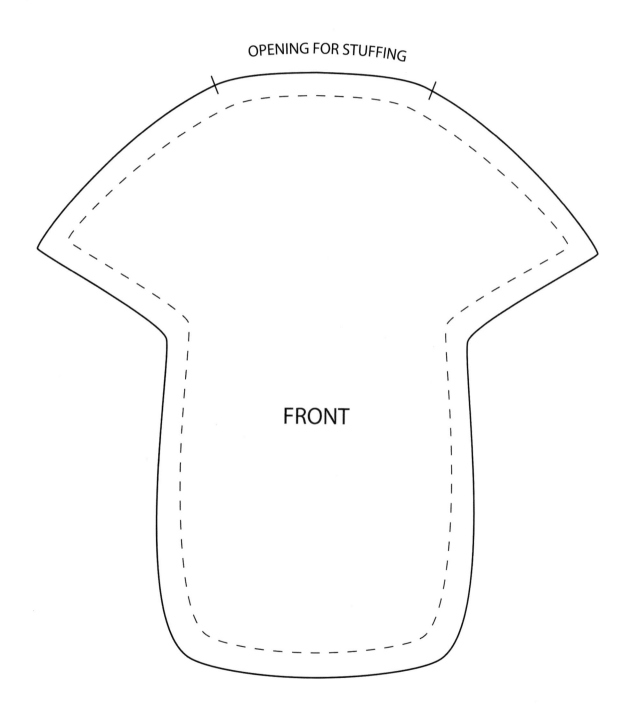

OPENING FOR STUFFING

FRONT

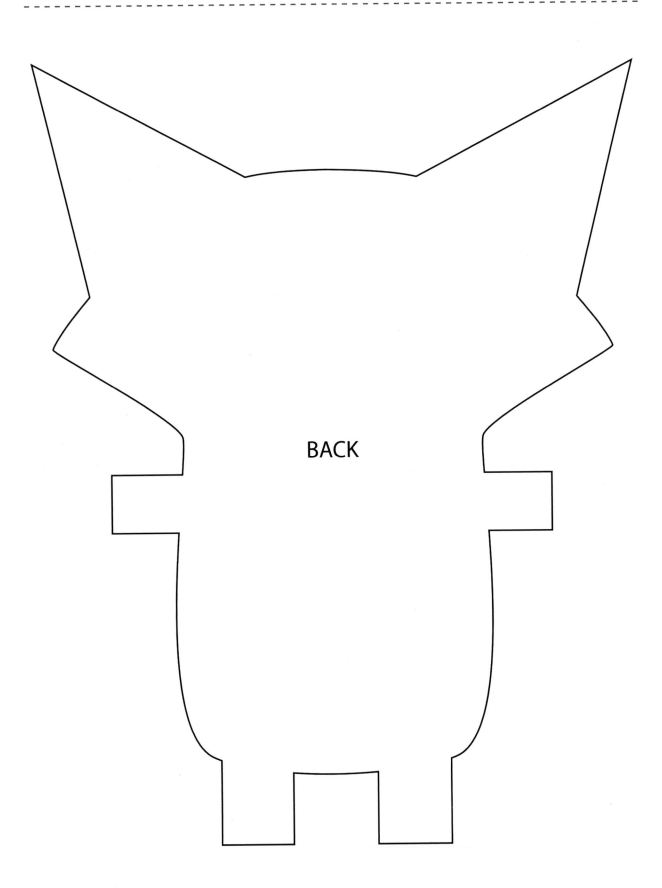

BACK

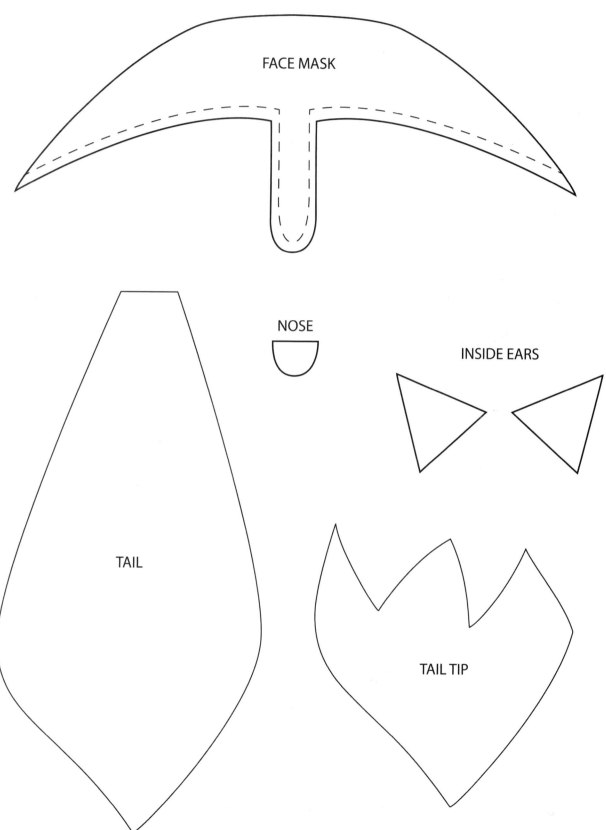

FACE MASK

NOSE

INSIDE EARS

TAIL

TAIL TIP

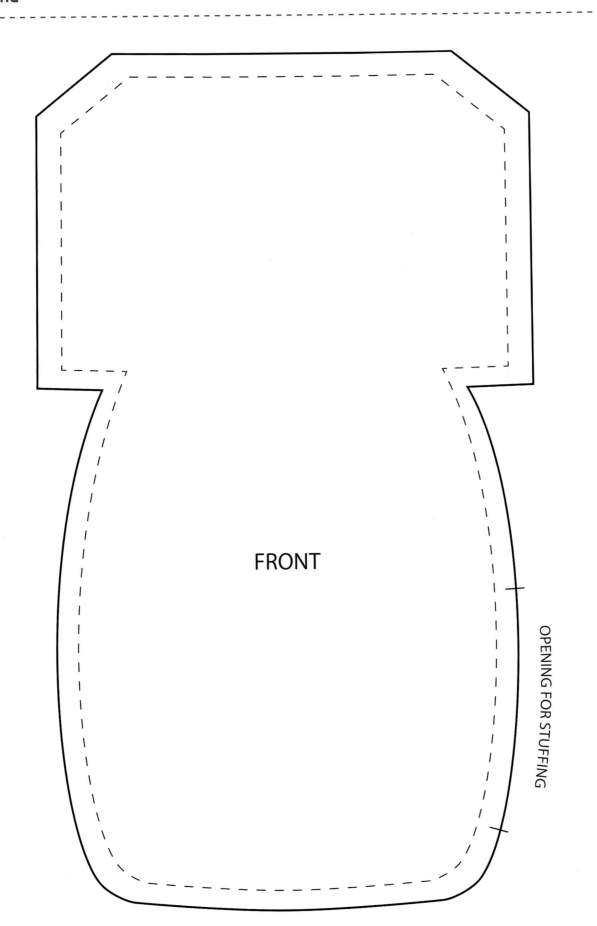

FRONT

OPENING FOR STUFFING

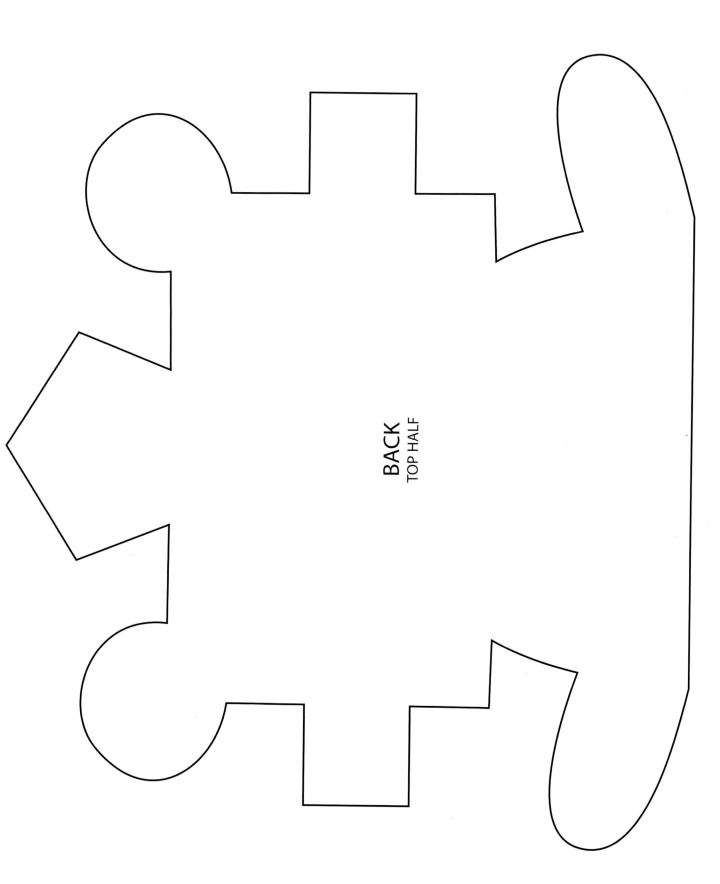

BACK
TOP HALF

Bella

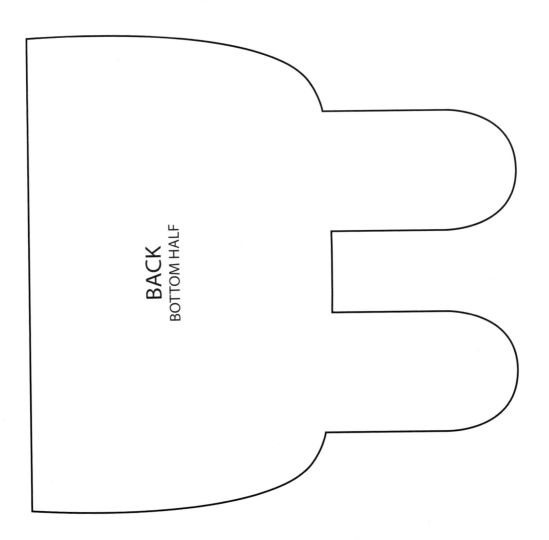

BACK
BOTTOM HALF

INSIDE EARS

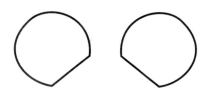

NOSE

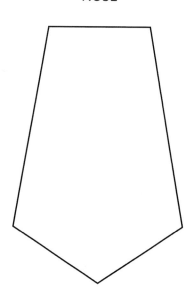

NOSE TIP

"MY SON, NICHOLAS, IS 9 AND HAS NEVER BEEN PATIENT ENOUGH TO SEE A SEWING PROJECT THROUGH TO THE END . . . UNTIL TODAY! HE WAS SURPRISED THAT HE WAS ABLE TO DO IT BY HIMSELF AND KEPT SAYING, "I CAN'T BELIEVE IT . . . THIS WAS JUST SOME FABRIC AND I DID THIS!!"

—MOM OF NICHOLAS, 9, PATTERN TESTER

MEET THE ZENKI PATTERN TESTERS

From top, L to R
Alyssa, 17, USA
Alexander, 10, Australia
Aneeka, 7, Australia
Alice, 13, USA
Amelie, 8, Australia
Anna, 9, UK
Cammie, 9, USA
Colton, 10, USA

From top, L to R
Caoimhe, 9, Ireland
Charlotte, 7, USA
Celeste, 13, Australia
Sofia, 13, Italy
Nicholas, 9, Italy
Cara, 9 & Katie, 11, Ireland
Dani, 10, USA
Ellie, 10, USA

From top, L to R

Elmarie, 10, South Africa

Elyse, 8, Australia

Evie, 4, Canada

Grace, 12, USA

Gracie, 10, USA

Grace, 7, UK, with Cookie,
 5 minutes old

Finley, 9, Canada

Freddie, 6, Australia

"I WAS EXCITED
ABOUT THE PATTERN.
I WAS PROUD
OF THE CREATION."

—KEIRA, 8,
PATTERN TESTER

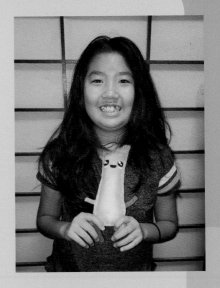

From top, L to R
Isla, 10, UK

Amelia, 7, Australia

Jessica, 12, USA

Joel, 5, USA

Jana, 8, Saudi Arabia

Josie, 6, USA

Jonty, 8, UK

Ruby, 8, USA

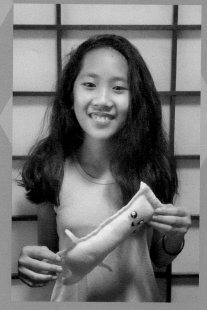

From top, L to R

Katie, 11, Canada

Kaylee, 11, USA

Kyra, 9, USA

Lily, 9, UK

Marti, 8, Spain

Noralie, 15, USA

Maxim, 9, Canada

Rory-Jane, 11, Australia

From top, L to R
Julia, 9, Canada
Karen, 12, USA
Kate, 9, USA
Kate, 16, USA
Sophie, 9, USA
Tom, 8, UK
Edie, 9, England
Makenna, 12, USA

From top, L to R
Syndhl, 8, USA
June, 8, USA
Jillian, 11 & Rosetta, 8, USA
Wylly, 10, USA
Hadassah, 11, Canada
Keira, 8, Australia
Ellie, 10, USA
Sophia, 11, England

TRiXi SYMONDS is the founder of the worldwide sew-together phenomenon Sew a Softie, which has been featured in *Simply Sewing, Homespun, Handmade, Casa Creativa, Love Patchwork and Quilting, Little U* from *Uppercase,* and many more.

A designer and teacher with over 25 years' experience, Trixi has held workshops in Kyoto, Amsterdam, and Melbourne, and in venues all over her home city of Sydney, including the Art Gallery of NSW, the Museum of Contemporary Art, and the Australian Museum.

She was asked to design a simple-to-sew Ugly Doll by the promoters of the UK release of the *Ugly Dolls* movie and designed a piranha softie for Aaron Blabey's book *Piranhas Don't Eat Bananas.*

Her other books include *Sew Together Grow Together,* which offers 20 hand-sewing projects that bring parents and children together through sewing, and *Sewing Simple Softies with 17 Amazing Designers,* coauthored with Deborah Fisher.
www.sewasoftie.com